Face Me: a declaration

Face Me:
a declaration

Olivia Keenan

for my sisters

Contents

i.
exposition

click

click

There is a suspicious man in the parking lot. I lock the car doors. I avoid eye contact. I walk past the mall kiosks with my head down. I take the freeway into the city. I hold my breath when I get cat-called. In other words, the man in the parking lot is Black. And I happen to be afraid of who I am.

click.

I skip past the SOCIAL MEDIA STORIES THAT EXHIBIT HIS DEATH LIKE THIS IS SHOWTUNES SHOWBIZ SHOWCASE US LIKE THIS IS EASY FOR US LIKE THIS IS EASY FOR MY FOURTEEN YEAR OLD SISTER. I can't even breathe WATCHING THAT SHIT.

click.

I flip through more stories. People are posting SILENCE IS VIOLENCE.

I type, re-type, delete.

"as a Black girl..."

I haven't said anything yet and therefore I must be a part of the problem. And I don't know how to say it is so HARD, it is so HARD to say something besides from PLEASE when you can't breathe.

click.

I imagine guns in the cars that blast the same music me and my white friends listen to. Me and my white boyfriend's breath fogs the car windows. Silver tinted. If we get pulled over we'll get a slap on the wrist. Shiny cars fly down the roads. Me and my white friends like to speed on the parkway with the windows down.

click.

Right now I am afraid for (of?) my city and my country. There are red white and blue flags being snatched out of the ground. There are red white and blue lights and sirens and I close my bedroom window. There are red white and blue popsicles in the freezer. That's an onomatopoeia. Pop. In suburbia, we hold out our fingers like a sideways "L".

click.

pop.

click.

I skip past the news because all I ever see about Black boys is all I ever see about Black boys. And all porn says is BBC and all sports say is athlete and all the papers say is death and all the news says is riot and then I lock the car doors. Then I take the freeway. Then I avoid eye contact. Then I blame myself.

click,

I press play. I watched the video tonight. Because there's only so many times you can skip past it before you see.

breathe, please.

Let ME. Breathe PLEASE.

I breathe in. I hold my breath when I get catcalled. My kid sister can't even breathe watching that shit. Now all I can say is that I'm glad I don't have kid brothers because no one would ever suffocate her (right?). I breathe out. Me and my breath fogs the windows. I write "I CAN'T BREATHE" into the dew.

I eat all the red white and blue popsicles and throw up the american flag. The ground is speckled with holes: where the flags used to be. I sing a song about the hood and take the freeway to pass it. My white friends say fuck the police and I wonder if they have ever been afraid of them, too.

I kneel at church and my knees burrow into the floor. I am suffocating someone while praying for good grades or some shit. The ground says PLEASE and I kneel harder. I keep breathing.

HOW do I say this?

I feel like a problem. I lock the car doors. Again. Again. CLICK. CLICK. CLICK. The man in the parking lot pounds on my window.

CAN YOU BREATHE IN THERE.

Maple Tree Ln,
Brookfield WI 53045

I apologize for scaring the family of scarecrows

But how does a crow compare to the whole cornfield?

I am in their crosshairs, cornered

Young boys are being raised to be just like their fathers

The black crows compare to the whole cornfield

much like how black stalks along the borders of daytime

Young boys are being raised to be just like their fathers

They know enough about nature to know what's right and what's
black

like the way Black girls stalk along the suburb border and curbsides

It doesn't matter if I live two streets down,

the Watch knows enough about nature and black birds and rightness

Curly haired girls have apologies prewritten on bruised wrists

It never mattered where I lived! (two streets down)

It doesn't matter that my car was polished or that it is high noon

Cross haired Black girls pre-write their apologies with wrists turned
up,

as soon as young boys pedal by, just like their fathers

It doesn't matter where my car was parked or how quietly I croon.

I am cornered, and they ask me what I'm doing here, anyway.

Questions peddled by young boys, they watch me with their father's
eyes

I apologize, to seven year old scarecrows, for the existence of black things two streets down.

I surrender

in suburbia, I am walkable.

which is to say, I am easy to walk upon.

even God knows the way my chest feels against His feet.

in suburbia, I mince my words.

if this were weather, my words would be dust storms, words dust

I sweep dust into the garbage cans.

in suburbia, I am a caricature.

I am the wind obeying the weatherman.

I know how to play the part of a picture perfect Black girl.

in suburbia, I surrender.

which is to say, if this were weather, I am the wind obeying the whiteman

even God knows I sweep my words to play the part.

March. Again.

In the city, March is the cruellest month.
The drive to church is a straight shot.

Start on snow-plowed suburban roads with CHILDREN AT PLAY signs
salted sidewalks, no streetlights. Because nothing lurks
in the dark here,
in the night of a winter that never ends.

The snow plugs the spring closed
atop pot-holes that polka dot the roads,
today the winter never felt so slow.

There is a man on the sidewalk yelling
at God. It is Sunday, after all, and it is still so cold.

Yesterday it warmed up,
revealing the secrets of summer we wished were hidden.
Like THIS is where suburbia ends and begins to turn,
where the slice of yellow PAYDAY LOANS signs start to burn

oh March, you are cruel and you knew this would happen.
You knew we wanted green and would get grey instead, here
where the dark people live
where we keep the streetlights on,
where we pretend that spring is here
and the cold doesn't hurt.

Watch the shivering children wait for a bus that will never come.
skipping stones and dreams along the cold street shoulder
Watch the expectant, frozen breath of the city collect above our
heads.
At least the snow covered up everything before,
at least the winter kept guns silenced, skewed bullets.
March reminds the city how to shoot a straight shot.

One block away and the windows have bars.

Doesn't do much to keep the cold out.

There is a restlessness in the snow melt gasoline stream

alongside the road side

a flickering ticking in the streetlights.

The car turns, sighs, scrapes the air as it drives

We are here and we step out into the unforgiving air.

There are sirens in the distance and I don't even notice them.

Inside the warmth of mass, I can't remember the yelling man;

It is Sunday, after all, and I don't remember to pray.

virgin blues

I kiss boys behind blue lockers and let them press me against blue tile walls as soon as I get breast buds.

I bloom beyond summertime, beyond prepubescent heartbreak. It turns out that the blues bleed.

I eat all the blueberries his mom gives us in a blue clay bowl he made.

I kiss with full blue-stained lips and we drive home in bent silence.

I give backseat blowjobs tucked into the seconds before curfew. Yet, I am the one who always has blue balls.

I wear a blue dress and my father is the only one who calls me beautiful.

I kiss him under blue disco lights, on top of sagging bar floors, he bites my neck until it bleeds.

I let him call me beautiful, but walk home with bruises and buds and blueberries.

I go to his room, he bumps LED lights from soft to dark blue. I ask if he is angry with me.

I watch his face fade into blue shadows, a stretched out bird he blooms, boxers abandoned.

I tell him I don't want to see that: beaked boy all bent and beckoning. He asks if I am angry with him.

I leave. I never was good at being the bluebird with the buzz, the boys, I mean bees, I mean backseats.

I forget to button my blouse when I climb into blue cars. My driver asks me my age. I bluff.

I keep my finger up in Never Have I Ever and blush.

I still apologize to God every day, messages in balloons I let go into the blue breeze.

I suppose I wish for more than what I am sorry for. So I blow. Blue dandelion fuzz. The blue buds bleed.

I paint my nails blue, like the sky; they are so long I have to type with the pads of my fingers.

I won't cut them. I don't even want to touch myself anymore.

lucky who?

I learn how to extend myself
without exposing myself

I unfasten my pants,
but not before warning him of the caveats

I close my eyes when I am spread apart;
disclaimers taste sweet on a weathered tongue

if you cry and tell the boys 'wolf' enough times
they will believe you for real.

how is it that I open up
with legs all criss crossed?
all motionless and motioning?
all tense and trembling?

feet in the air, I point my toes to distract myself
count to 400, so at 401
I fake it, point my toes harder,
cry 'i'm there!' and 'wolf!' and 'i'm sorry!' and

he washes his hands of me.
he does not accept my apology.

lucky who?
we've got red scrubbed hands and red scrubbed lips
raw skin and blue balls and sweet soap, a shamed kiss

amidst my caveated uncovering
disclosed displayal
I count to arbitrary numbers.
there is dirt under his fingernails.

I do not feel lucky.

white boys still don't let me
sign the damn declaration of
independence

in my dreams I worship you, jefferson
I wake up and find you in 21st century soccer boys

in my dreams my friends burn your statue and erase your epitaph
and I fight it, and I *fight* it, and I ask to give you a second chance
and there are red rings on my ankles
and everyone says "what the *fuck* are you doing??? you *know* what
he's done!!!
he does not want you the way that you are"

but this is how I am to be liberated, like the lines
in your equality notes
oh, baby, oh

yes.   fetishize me, founding father.
call me american dream and fuck me until I call you   america,
america back.

I will sign your big name on the bottom
with my hand around your cock, sealed promise
of freedom,   for you only

but if I could just have a chance to show you how I can please you
while tied up, while shackled, while bound, while gagged, while
strewn out, I will worship you if it means I can become you and sign
the damn thing
too

but either way I will call you father. either way I will call you history. either way I will call you God. either way I will scour for you in basement parties and tie my hair up and reassure you I am a carrier for blue eyes.

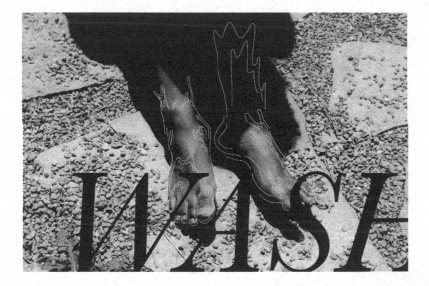

wash.

And there was a woman in the city who was a sinner

she began to wash his feet with her tears

It sure is easy to be a sinner   nowadays

I, born sinning, sinner born,

wash his feet with my worn hands

In the city, there is a sinner, and it is me

I cry sometimes, but only for the washing

out of us: one is a city, the other a Black girl

the former does not wash feet.

(that is not how the story goes but it is how it is)

washer born, I kneel in veneration.

in this story, I never stop cleansing his feet

he is not god (right?) but He is somebody's son

and redemption sounds sweet when he speaks of it.

old wars on old couches

white boys like it when I wear clothes that slide off easy
bare boned in bluelight basements
I clothe myself in television glares and splayed fingers.
when he looks at me,
I pray naked bodies can be wanted
even when Black.

oh, *please*. fetishize me. founding father.

you are the one who taught me how to fight revolutions
you gave me sneak peeks into the signing rooms
I smelled freedom on your ink spotted fingertips

when he holds me, he is careless, and it is I who smells like freedom.
(can you sense the irony on my ironclad body?)

I let him pull my hair back, expose my neck
submission is a small price to pay for liberation
If enough of them lend their weapons, I'll take whoever's next!

now we got all these unarmed Black girls on battlegrounds
I didn't know I had to fight old wars on old couches
lit up by screens, I watch the credit scenes skate over my skin
speckled by words and white fingers, white flags, no wins

history repeats. The wars unfolded on sofas were pre-won,
facades are funny. The movie's done.

This is the Queen of the

this is the queen of

back row so the other kids don't have to see past afros or the past
or afros

of the pigtails and ponytails and permanent updos

of being the only one in all the rooms

of the front rows, too, but hunchbacked and doubled over, so they
see the back of afros

of singed hair straighteners, and red rimmed ear lobes

of split ends and trim refusals, so the other kids will stop calling me
MJ

of tangles on the bathroom tiles and dry shampoo bottles

of daydreams, in which I sit up straight, like daydream hairdos

of barrettes and beads and brown and black and the in-betweens

queen of the other kids, because I've convinced them I'm theirs

queen of convincing myself, too.

queen of ponytails. queen of being the only one. queen of all the rooms.
queen of heads and heat. queen of seeing past myself and the past in
myself. queen of queen of the back row. queen of burned ear lobes.
queen of the other side. not a green queen. a daydream queen. tangles
and beads queen. queen of reaching. queen of convincing. queen of the
in between. queen of.

Non-Reciprocation

I swallow my ancestors when I am with him.
Which is to say, we do not talk about race.
These white boys never mention that I'm Black
as if I can't feel my own body's Blackness
when he partakes in non-reciprocation

I swallow my history, spit out the remains.
This new mouth of mine is what freedom tastes like
receiving, agreeing, pleading,
If he will hold me in silence, I will silence myself
If he will hold me
If he will hold me

It turns out that I hate myself. I hang myself
from white boy belt loops
so that I am close by
When we partake in his favorite part of non-reciprocation
I think THIS is what freedom tastes like
shame and semen, my mustache white
I daydream of sweet day releases
consummated liberty, savory birthrights

yes,   Yes,   YES!
fetishize ME, founding father!!

I can and I will do anything for you
eyes locked, bent over, standing up,
I will swallow whatever you need me to!!!

Me and Jefferson

at the conclusion of streaking the Lawn, one must run up the Rotunda steps and whisper into the keyhole of the Rotunda door (where you start and end your streak), saying "Goodnight, Mr. Jefferson". That man built this school!

Goodnight, Mr. Jefferson
(that's what I say when I'm done streaking)
with my lips pressed against the keyhole, I whisper...
Mr. Jefferson, no peeking

bare boned against brick buildings
this was always how you'd first see me
you'd sweep my clothes under the dirt, say—
this was always how you'd prefer to greet me
got all these naked Black girls on your sacred grounds
but you forget to mention that in your stories
got all these unarmed Black girls on your battlegrounds
scratch that out of your declaration of liberty
bare boned against night breath
I become clothed by starlight and column shadows

this was always when you'd promise to free me.
And I'd say yes, free me
I'd say yes, see me
I'd say yes
fetishize me, founding father.

call me american dream and fuck me until I call you america,
america back.
because in my dreams I bow to you, Jefferson

I wake up and find you in 21st century soccer boys
american stripe blue eyes, this nation under God prayers
tell me I look better under you
than next to you
on your parent's dinner chairs

smashed lips against my mouth
I thought this was what freedom tastes like
you said there is no time to taste me
for I must be what captivity tastes like

it's funny — this is how I am to be liberated,
you are how I am to be liberated, like the lines in your equality notes
oh baby, oh
you like it when I call you Father. you like it when I call you Savior.
you like it when I call you God.

allegiance pledged, I would scour for you as I ran uncovered
grass and wind robes, moonlit exposed
traipsing naked, unshaven, down your well groomed lawn,
I thought that you, Jefferson, could un-enslave me
that you could suck the quill tip, scrawl in my signing,
as if your words could step up and save me, this glass bone baby
alas, I obliged.

I would call you founding father, God among men, history definer
call me dead, call me   call me   call me   call me

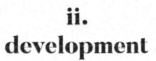

ii.
development

stained glass girls

upon walking into the sanctuary,
sunlight stipples the tiled floor,   the rising gray dust,   the
hymnal covers
          sunday mourning,   my mind is flush of lust
          I must   take in   the church gospel
                but I stick my fingers into the font and suck on them
I peer heavy-lidded at   stained glass images of genesis   and
                          the world's First Time
          the eve in our Black church windows has   sunlight skin
she is naked
          save for green petals of streaked glass   tiger lily
covered breasts
    her red apple rays dapple my open palms   red understanding on
her
          fingertips,
    as well as mine
the garden moistens parched lips   this is Knowledge.
in sin-free eden   she even eats what I need her to
          nibbles lush honey crisp seeds   looks up at satan with
give-it-to-me
          eyes   covers her naked bones in lingerie   and falls
    buncha Black Girls in the windows   too   (kidding)
          this is a Black church   but eve turns the floors
salmon
      this is a Black church   and yet our bibles are white,
and our God too
in other words   the windows said woman got pink lady pussy
    I wish the windows said she danced
                that her hair grew in zigzags like phone cords
          I wish eve got sum melanin   this sum
sunkissed sin
      cuz amidst all these scenes of peach fuzz and peach skin

I've got bruised lips   barbed bikini line   brown stubble pelvis
bent tresses
    birthmarks look like someone was there before,   oh creator of all
tell me I can be the woman in these rainbow stories
            tell me I got that Knowledge too   tell me I Falled
I will bathe in the fountain's colored waters   collect golden
ripples on
            my curves
    and   sprinkle them into the eyes of parishioners
I will   bleed ebony into pews   pray with probing hands   procure
with my
            palate.
            oh, creator of all   feed me glass apple seeds
like aphrodisiac eve   I will dip my red tongue into the core
and swallow it

Chapter 1 Verse 1

genesis bliss   call me afro-head discotheque eve

  if it were my window   the fruit would have been a raisin

  all violet and soft and sundried   I would have shown it to eden

would have said   take this, and eat it   I know you want

knowledge   and this jazz pussy

virgin Blacks

I kiss white boys behind black lockers and they tell me they like me because of my demeanor.

I bloom into an apology-- this dark girl's become a master of dignity. Which is to say, I find out I'm Black.

I eat all the blackberries we pick along the side paths on the parkway.

I kiss with full Black berried lips and we drive home in bent silence.

I give backseat blowjobs tucked into the seconds before curfew. Even in the dark no one wants to confront my Blackness.

I wear my Black hair down and my father is the only one who calls me beautiful.

I pretend that I'm done with white boys, but bump into them on purpose in dark frat basements.

I hold a beer can above my head when I dance. I play a game called One-Sided Eye Contact with Chad.

I kiss whoever asks under disco lights, on top of sagging bar floors. Whoever Asks is never white.

I let him call me beautiful, but walk home with Black hair and blackberries.

I have never gone home with a Black boy. He asks me if I've ever been high before. I tell him I am a virgin. In many ways.

I watch his face fade into shadows as like a stretched out bird he blooms, boxers abandoned.

I tell him I don't want to see this. Not like this. So he tries to see me next. But I am bent knees and fig leaf fingers. He asks me if I am angry with him.

I never was good at being the blackbird with the buzz, I mean bees, I mean boys, I mean Black. So I leave.

I jump over fences to get to my ride. My blouse is still unbuttoned and my driver and I pretend it isn't. We both bluff.

I keep my finger up in Never Have I Ever and blush.

I apologize to God every day, prayers left in the shuffled sheets of near one night stands.

I suppose I wish for what I am not. So I leave. Black boy beds. My blackberried body bleeds.

I close my Black eyes when I get out of the shower. I turn off the lights and break all the mirrors. I sleep with my arms above my head.

I happen to be afraid of who I am.

I can't even touch myself anymore.

lucky you

I know that we both
have our prayers for the dark.
I can feel the rushed whispers
to God brush against my skin. call
and response. we both say
"I'm sorry" but, it's not you,
it's me. maybe He'll understand
if we all apologize for my
body. someday I will ask us
to say our prayers aloud. maybe
then you will tell me the
Truth. maybe then you will bite into
the fruit. maybe then I won't have
to close my eyes so I don't
have to see yours closed,
too.

lucky. our God seems to really get you.

scripture and shame entangled
in my sheets, it has always been
easy for you to leave.
you are not the one who
begs for forgiveness at
the end of the night. my hands
emptied yet this bed still holds
my trespasses, my trespassers,
the evil one, the gatekeeper.
let anybody in. let anybody
out. there are some things
that God cannot forgive us for
and I am afraid I am one of them.

hi, yellow!

enter in the morning sky, gently spilling on my face
yellows soak my skin in the early hours
I bask in marigold hues, I am dark bread buttered

The yellow sun rises,
yellow high, highest
call me the sun, then
lemon meringue lifted above the mahogany table
I am the dessert saved for the guests
light enough for them to swallow
sweet and spicy enough to digest

hi, yellow!
I say to the morning
I cradle light in my hands and rub it
across my body

yellow an elixir, yellow my ticket to ride,
yellow my shame, my glory yellowed
yellow my n-word pass, yellow my inflections
the check boxes yellow on my college applications,
my acceptances yellowed, my acceptance yellowed
yellow a liberation, yellow my giveaway
yellow my exclusion, yellow my Black,
yellow my yellow my prayers my prayers
my prayers yellow

if he don't like too much color, maybe he'll still like me
hi, hello!
you take sun beams to bed?
you feel less sorry around me?
you hungry enough for honey glazed girls?

how mellow!
yellow girl can laugh off the Black jokes

yellow girl can take it
yellow girl can take it
isn't she white enuf to understand
what yellow does for her??
yellow girl rubs all that yellow on her skin every morning!
calls it cleaning
calls it denial
calls it routining

but high yellow girls learn quickly
this yellow sheen is deceiving

plessy yellows are still fucken Black

Black on Black

It's a numbers game, really.
If there are two of us, they'll surely take one.
They will need a brochure baby
to be in the photographs--
Black beauty show-horse on the front page.
I groom myself to be the fastest
so that I can be the one.
I don't care if they parade me
on pamphlets or promises.
It is a Black on Black crime
in my interview.
I tell them why it is I who deserves to be here
when there were two of us in the waiting room.

It's a numbers game, really.
If you are the only one, they
still won't want you.
In the limited light, I am liminal.
Black beauty made it to the front page
but won't find a husband here.
They think my hair makes me look like a boy.
So I tie my hair up when I talk to boys.
Tied up and tucked back when I talk to boys.
It's a Black on Black crime
when I go to frat parties.
I tell them that unlike my hair, I can be tamed,
but they still won't call me by my name.

It's a numbers, game, really!!
who kills more Black people, really?!?!?!
I see my first city shooting on TV,
the first of many, of many.
Downtown a homeless man approaches my stopped car.

I tuck dollar bills in between the car seats
and crevices and claim cashlessness.
It's a Black on Black crime
when I watch the news.
If I tell you where I live, we both know it's the suburbs.
That's where Black on Black crime gets the most views.

I breathe in hallowed breaths
count the deaths on a thousand fingers
the air thick with blame and I am sucking all of it in
In my interview, I tell them why I want to be here,
but all I want is to be held.
In my interview, in my interview,
I know the news. I passed that
man on the way here,
too. It's a numbers game, really.
I just want you to call me by my
name, really. If you pick me,
I'll pose in your pictures! I,
Black beauty, apologize for the Race.
Ask me what came first... the Black people
or the crime? Force my hand,
I'll say what you want, white lies,
I will win the race: a numbers game.
The game numbers, and my interviewers
score me slowly. They are the ones who
decide the victors, anyway.

Compromising

most nights
my glass is three-fifths full

you really respect three-fifths of a person?
I ask him, between sips of white wine
he, the one who wants white wives,
says he will take me cuz he is color blind
but afraid to touch me

    1. the point is, you didn't correct me.

you ready to hold three-fifths of my body tonight?
I ask him, through slow swaying and solos
bent backs, bunched up clothes,
stripped skin, nighttime compromise!
he, who calls me sexy,
says he'll take me cuz I act like the [white] wine in my cup

    2. I KNOW!!! HOW TO DO!!! FUCKING FRACTIONS!!!
    (I'll accept any command to get my two parts back)

you understand what I mean?
I ask him. YOU have what I need
he, who crunched the numbers anyway,
says he'll take me because he is color blind and I am also white
wine— desperate for full cups, and he doesn't have to touch me to
get the job done.

    3. say it. SAY IT.
    just like the constitution, you are a fucking coward!!!   SAY IT.
    give it to me ! I can take it !

Hands up

hands up !
I am going to be the largest being being

hands up!
hallelujah! we praise God with our prayers in the air anyway

hands up!
I am going to be the largest being being

hands up!
the boys and girls grow up. the boys and girls GROW UP.
HANDS UP! BLACK GROWN UPS COMING IN
COMING THROUGH BLACK BEINGS BEING HANDS UP

HALLELUJAH.

lilac Gods

I named you BOYFRIEND
It is May and my fantasy boyfriend
rises from the lilac bushes
like a baptism and I am baptised.
My Heavenly Father is 6'3" with crooked middle fingers
He has a nice car and that is what he names you— Nice Car.
He drives under broken streetlights
sticky stick shift hands steer the shots
and if an accepting open mouth will canonize me,
I will worship the purple sundown reflecting in his eyes
I will thank him for the night, and what he painted
when he disappears (long after the lilacs have wilted)
I will still pray to him

I named you GOD
It is May. Again.
and I think that at last I got it right
I memorize scripture
(the real kind!)
I sing a bunch of praise songs
with a bunch of white people
They tell me the Church needs
"more people like me"
but I am not like you,
am I?
praising you with them feels like
choking (similar to BOYFRIEND)
sitting in pews makes me horny
and so I apologize
(for being horny)
my clit is purple because blue balls.
when I touch myself
I apologize beforehand

and we agree not to talk about it ever again
In this church I am not sweating
but surely I have sinned,
shivering, and I wonder if heaven is cold
the sermon says that those who don't
"know" you, GOD
are damned, GOD damned
Some people name you Hell.
I do not know you, GOD
it is May and the lilacs are blooming
and I forget about purple again
Plus,
I like it when they
call me condemned.

I write with your name on my tongue
It was given to you at my birth,
(HEAVENLY FATHER/MOTHER EARTH)
the taxonomy is mine to claim
I pinpoint PURPLE on every page
I, EVEn, rose from rib cages,
I named you first.

May comes again. At last.

I do not name you aloud this time.
And it is now that I begin to understand.
The lilacs did not bloom this year
but I hold you in my arms
I apologize to my purpled body
and we heal it together
Next year the bloom will be better
It was payback for calling you BOYFRIEND.

I read the declaration of independence anyway

In your arms but, my body was scrapped,   we

do not stay parked for long, when you   hold

my hands, you shake, we both know   these

two languages we speak will reveal the   Truths

someday, someday soon, let us not forget   to

close my eyelids, after I've gone, you will   be

revered, you write with precedent pens, my   self:

I bleed in the margins, in the shadows,   evident-

ly left on the sorry roadside, discarded so   that

when they read it, it will be clear who this   all

has been written for anyway, thumbs bent,   Men

do not stop as they go past, I know they   are

readers, and that they know what you   created

in the white spaces in   between,   equal

calluses

my hair's been beat up ever since I could muster fists
tough palms and rough tresses,
it takes a lot of hair brushing to make me cry

I set tired eyes on the cameras
but still free fervor from cages
(what is this fear you speak of? I've got hardened skin)

I am the callused queen of heads and heat
christened in curls, criss cross tangles
If I believed something else back then,

I've convinced myself otherwise.
now I daydream in mirrors, with widened eyes.

awash

when I am included within what I believe in,

the universe imitates me.

caught some of my skin for sunlight

curly haired bush bramble

brown eyed skies got reflections for stars

awash, wash me in love, dear God, dear Universe, dear dear dear

call me by my name, call me by yours, call me by ours

I know the secret because it is inside me.

when I am included within what I believe in,

I am a queen, the washer, the washed.

born sinner feet cleaned, so

somebody's son got on his knees,   too

said "let me share this kingdom with you"

when I am included within what I believe in,

when I AM INCLUDED within what I believe in,

Black girls awash with believing

awash with seeing,

truth on our tongues,

awash.

iii.
recapitulation

I compose myself

I compose myself into composure. Hold my posture. It is my choice to be composed. This does not make me mild mannered. This does not make me gentle. This does not make me feeble.

I compose myself into thoughts. We all have questions. It is my choice to explain myself. This does not make me the answer to all answers. This does not make me wrong. This does not make me wavering.

I compose myself into music. This is what I've always been. It is my choice to become poetry. This does not make me sorry. This does not make me shifty. This does not make me salt pillars.

I compose myself into hallelujah. My hands raise up, up, up. At last, there is no surrendering. Here, I am praising. Being. With upturned praying palms. I compose

myself.

who is that in the protests?

masked mothers prop cooing babies on their hips / through passing
car windows I see young ones peeking past dashboards / A VOICE
CALMS THOSE OF ALL THE CHILDREN

they are kneeling on the cracked concrete / crayon colored signs
raised with the sun / A HAND HOLDS UP THOSE OF ALL
THE CHILDREN

little girls and boys lift heavy fists / they sit at the head of the
protest / THEY POOL AT HIS FEET

they stream into the streets / they gaze at Him with childlike
wonder / WE HAVE NEVER BEEN MORE WONDERFUL

there was a flood before,

look at how History repeats itself

the children's deluge

baptism in their voices

I am reborn in the masses

we are all masked but our God is maskless

there is a Third who always walks beside us

Sonata for my Sisters

my momma hair so big the doorway has to get out of her way

my sister hair so frizzy the umbrella uses her to stay dry

my cousin hair so wild the shower drain says HELL NAH

my dad head so bald yet he always grumbling about the SHOWER DRAINS!

goddamn

it rains hair in this home!!

you ever seen hair stop weather?   you ever been around a Black girl?

we catch the clouds in our manes—

call it curly, call it nappy, call it magic

call it sunshine— our hair catches that too

rays turn to gold on every curl

can the other girls do that???

no, ma'am

those people use real umbrellas

we harnessed the rain centuries ago

ii.

my lips so big I kiss the sky without meaning to

my lips so wide I pull waves when I wake

my lips so soft, like the dawn, sun rays splay

my mouth paradise— beach balm glistenin

you should sit in here and start listenin

pressed against your ears, I whisper with the oceans

"   *goddamn*   "

you ever kissed lips like this?

I hold the seas in my grips   call it choppy, call it smooth, call it magic

call it gusty,   my lips blow that too

sea foam salt and riptide sugar caught on my tongue

can the other girls do that???

no, ma'am

I breathe like seashells and host hurricanes in my hips

my Black body got big lips everywhere

iii.

my momma soul so big she don't have time to make supper

my sister soul so strong she got Atlas grumbling about THIS BITCH

my soul so shiny I've been teaching the sun how to pray

my dad soul so full cuz he got four Black girls to hold

goddamn

you get it now? we came out dancing we came out music we came
out rhythm

soul music in our flat and natural movements

call it slap-happy call it wishbones call it overcome (overcame!) call
it magic

you ever believed in God for real?   you ever loved a Black girl?

we the sunshine and the sea

we the kingdom and all the queens

can the other girls do that?

no ma'am

If I am the sonata, this my recapitulation

I harnessed the reins centuries ago

my Black body coded codas, da capo

princess mobutu

when I was seven I wanted to be a princess, too / so my mother created princess mobutu

**pre-princess-tiana girls / gen-z-coconut-pigtail girls / television-forgotten-millenium-cusp-born girls / 9/11-baby-and-still-no-dark-baby-dolls girls /

I gotchu

call me mobutu / means whatever you need it to / these girls don't have a mother language / your mother made me up to make up for a motherland and lack thereof / I am from where you are from

none of this sleeping beauty-type shit / I have been awake for 1000 years / none of this snow-white-type shit / I am coated in cocoa beans / none of this cinderella-type shit / I dance barefoot

I am not a slave / I repeat / I am not a slave / I am not a slave story / I am not enslaved to a story / my name in all the fairy tales / my garb in all the Halloween stores / I got constellations across the whole sky

I know how to cure generational self loathing / all my pages are black / all my words are black / no white shit dictates this book / every Black woman's name is written in the acknowledgments / how can you hate yourself now?

you get a princess in me! / you get a story in me! / you don't have to circle the whole continent when asked where you are from / you don't have to say "I'm sorry" when you can't answer where you are from

this is not english / you want a language? / my name syllabic / new speech / I speak in charismatic tongues / mobutu / moon bloom tune / bumotu / bloom moon tune / tumobu / tune moon bloom / you know what I mean, pre-princess tiana girl / the moon a black woman who sings when she rises / the tune a singing woman who rises from black moon/ the bloom! the bloom a moon woman rising to black songs

what I'm saying is / I gotchu / you come from somewhere / you are a descendant of royalty just like the other girls with stories / you are an ascendant of soul music and sixteenth notes and enslavery and sunday sabbath and goddamn. wait 'til they make a movie about us! / PRINCESS MOBUTU(S!) / you! get a story too**

lucky ME

I'VE FOUND
sitting criss cross applesauce still gives ME easy access
it takes some coaxing, but
it turns out there are no caveats between my legs
it turns out the wolves stay away if you stop calling for them (!!!!)
it turns out I don't need to say anything at the end,
except I'm there!! and this time, I am.

I'VE FOUND
that black kitties purr too, even when crossed
luck spills from heavy petting
there are rainbows in my pussy
ROYGBIV got comfortable
in between this wishbone pelvis

in fact, I'VE FOUND
it is not about luck when it comes to my body
Rename this poem FREEDOM AND FELICITY
Rename this poem DAILY SERENDIPITY
Rename this poem ME! TOUCHING ME!

I'VE FOUND
the only disclaimer I can give is
brace yourself! my self, my love, my lover
what a blessed place to be, what a blessing,
words will always do a disservice to my body
(falling short in their inaccuracy)
there is nothing more beautiful

than me in the midst of my finale.

Solomon's Song of Songs 6:10

"Has anyone ever seen anything like this [her]—
dawn fresh, moon-lovely, sun-radiant,
ravishing as the night sky with its galaxies of stars"

oh to be praising the Lord
and Her body in unison,
Solomon's psalms tucked deep within the gospels,
his musings are bookmarked in mine, oh,

it is now that I want to be in the Bible.
Has anyone ever seen anything like this (me)—
body drawn, I can be the dawn-fresh damsel
moonlit crescent curves full waist un-waned, got you un-weaned
sun queen, too sexy to be left out of scripture
enraptured kiss wisps of milky way, embodied celestial body
black galaxy girl got big lips everywhere

this a psalm then, too. this a song then, too.
hallelujah, Lord this is a song then, too.

oh Lord, if all praise of our bodies were also of you

Solomon's Song of Songs 4:11-12

"Your lips drop sweetness as the honeycomb,
my bride; milk and honey are under your tongue.
The fragrance of your garments is like the fragrance of Lebanon.
You are a garden locked up, my sister, my bride;
you are a spring enclosed, a sealed fountain."

honeycomb dipped against my lips for added sweetness,
my sisters, we braid milk and honey together with our tongues
blended from our sugar bones and whipped cream kisses
our fragrance the hum of brimming black bee nectar
the buzz of secret gardens, my sisters, my brides, my mothers, my
daughters
we are the sprinkle in springtime, sprung persephones
fountain of life sealed within our hips, sole epiphanies

This a psalm then too, this a song then too, Hallelujah, Lord.
This is a psalm then, too.

Solomon's Song of Songs 7:2-8

"Your navel is a rounded goblet that never lacks blended wine. Your waist is a mound of wheat encircled by lilies. Your breasts are the twin fawns of a gazelle. Your neck is an ivory tower. Your eyes are the pools of Heshbon by the gate of Bath Rabbim. Your nose is like the tower of Lebanon looking toward Damascus. Your head crowns you like Mount Carmel. Your hair is a royal tapestry; the king is held captive by its tresses. How beautiful you are and how pleasing, my love, with your delights! Your stature is that of the palm, and your breasts like clusters of fruit. I said, "I will climb the palm tree; I will take hold of its fruit."

Oh! You didn't believe me before that Solomon wrote these for ME?!

How do I say this??   No way Solomon wasn't in love with a Black girl.

My navel is the rounded rind of blended black wine. My waist, the tiger lillies and river valleys. My breasts are two fawns, while the world fawns at my feet. My neck is held so high, they built Babel to reach me. My eyes pool with stars, earthly constellations. My nose is a flock of free birds and all its wings. My 3C curls crown my caramel head with the gusto of lion manes, my hair is King of the jungle, holds the Kingdom in its reins. How beautiful you are, my sisters, how beautiful you are. You are.

Your stature was crafted in the palm of God, made in the image of you.

The earth says, "I will venerate you. I will take hold of your fruit and its juices, my daughters, my mothers, my brides, my sisters. My surface is the painting, but you are the muses."

This a psalm then too, this a song then too, Hallelujah, Lord. This is a psalm then, too.

I write myself in between the lines when America refused.

my hair in their Bible, my body in their Bible, my Black in their Bible

my Bible.

and so I run to you.

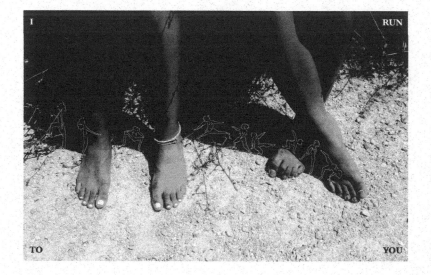

I run to you

When I tell our story, it begins with running,
closed books, and curved spinal cords; maybe I can dance
my way into heaven. the morning is young,
and I am early enough that I teach myself how to breathe
with it. night star swaddled, I always pray
with my palms face up, so at dawn we hold one

another. It is funny how children know the One
before the rest of us do, I do not know when running
to you became running to. I start to pray
with interlaced fingers, now-I-lay-me dancing
atop white knuckles and mismatched breathing,
remember when we used to breathe together, like young

loves, infant eyes glazed with awe, how eager and young
I was then, like the morning. during the day, the sun and the One
seem too separated to be on the same page, same breath,
if only I was created to look like you. then maybe I would run
to you. I kneel to the church, but here being Black moon is a dance
that won't get me into heaven. it is a good thing I don't like praying

to white people anyway. remember when I was born praying
palms up? the blue dawn breaks on Sunday, the young
morning gives a service to me: the moon, calls it a heavens dance,
how simple it is demonstrating rebirth when the One
is the sun, how simple it is to see you, once I stopped running
past sunskin and the new day, once I started calling myself the
moon, breathe

you in, out. my God the inhale, I the exhale, concerted breath,
moonlight on our fingertips, so many lights and prayers
to be held. my God color, my God upender of pews, my God ran
to me! bright God washes skin with holy hues, the young
son shows me how to close the book. after all, chapter one

is just the music and the moon and the morning. this dance
is all they do in heaven, anyway. I'll tell you my story: I dance
myself into the pages. my God's name in my breath,
my God Black joy while I am the exhalation. The One
comes running, palms face up so as to be held, pray
to me in return, the morning sun is young,

and at the edge of moon/sun, on the horizon, I run.

Me and Jefferson II

***at the conclusion of streaking the Lawn, one must run up the Rotunda
steps and whisper into the keyhole of the Rotunda door (where you start
and end your streak), saying "Goodnight, Mr. Jefferson". That man did not
build this school.***

tonight, Jefferson
dragging bare bones up the steps to reach the finish line,
I know about your feigned equality, sticky pinky swears of liberty
your freedom stars are stitched in old flags,
they unravel and every star in the sky becomes the northern one

and I wipe my upper lip and taste myself at last
and I bend over and sign the damn declaration of independence
fuck it, and I burn my clothes, the ones you buried
look at my battered body, born on your blessed grounds, birthday
suited

I am bare boned against the blue shadow buildings
brandished with Blackness, and I am freed
stripped Black girl on your battlegrounds says yes, see me, see me

FACE ME!

FOUNDING FATHER!

watch my blood run down the marble, into the cracks in the bricks
into the cobblestones, into raised Black fists
I coat myself in it, what you, god of men, forgot and left
in other words, I breathe at last

on your bloodied steps, in memory, in reverie,
history's souls rest in peace as I stand here now,
naked, consented, brazen
My signature smothers the whole page! This my recapitulation!
This my whole declaration!

Look what I can write, look how I can fight,
Look at my bold broken body in the Lawn light
All humans created equal, what a fucking sight

Mr Jefferson, goodnight

there is nothing more beautiful than me in the midst of my finale,
for I happen to be unafraid of who I am.

forgive me, but I have nothing to be forgiven for at the end of the
night.

un-caveated cries, I apologize for nothing

I take sun beams to bed!

I, born sinning, sinner born, awash with worn hands,

kiss with full blue-berried lips

so somebody's son had to get on his knees,   too.

in fact, my Black body got big lips everywhere!

moonlit crescent curves full waist unwaned, got the world
un-weaned,

sun queen is the buzz of secret gardens, sprinkle of springtime, I
braid milk and honey together with my tongues

I am the blackbird with the buzz and the bees;

I know enough about fighting and flying to take flight.

I, Black beauty, burn all the brochure pages

and even after I've gone, I am revered.

I have composed myself into music,

hallelujah,

I have remembered how to pray

Hallelujah! I praise God with my hands in the air anyway

I, Eve, rose from rib cages, and still I named you first.

My baptism in the voices, I am reborn in the masses,

I run at the edge of the horizons,

If this were weather, my words would be thunderstorms, words thunder

you ever seen hair stop weather?

you ever been in love with a Black girl?

daydream queen, in between queen

in all the mirrors, with widened eyes

so you can call me   call me   call me

call me afro-head discotheque eve, call me your majesty

my name syllabic!! new speech! I speak in charismatic tongues!!

I honor my ancestors when I am with him,

for they are the ones who taught me how to fight revolutions

no one needs to give it to me! I have already taken it!

I sign my big name on the bottom

write myself in between the lines when America refused,

face me founding father!
face me! face me! face me! face me! face me! face me! face me! face me!
face me!

References

All Bible verses in this book come from the New International Version English translation of the Bible.

Acknowledgements

As enjoyable of a process writing this book has been, it has taken a lot out of me. It would have not been completed without the continuous love and support I've received from my friends and family.

First of all, a special thanks to Carrie Severson for reaching out to my mom and I about writing. Without you, I would not have been able to get my voice out or work with the wonderful people in the Unapologetic Voice House.

Thank you as well to Kesiena Boom, my editor, who believed in me from the beginning. So much of what I love about this book comes from your help and advice.

A special thank you to Caroline Weis, who photoshopped all the pictures in this book. You did a stunning job, so thank you for lending your creative gifts to this project.

Thank you to my Milwaukee friends, who have been part of my original support circle since I started writing poems in seventh grade. Thank you for reading my bad middle school poetry and saying it was good!

Thank you as well to my Virginia friends, who have joined my support circle in the best ways possible. I am perpetually uplifted by "y'all" and with your help, have found myself and my faith in new ways.

Thank you to all my friends and teachers involved with me on my journey in poetry throughout the years. This means Wauwatosa West's English department, Wauwatosa West's slam poetry club, Milwaukee's

Stillwaters Collective, UVA's Flux Poetry club, my CUPSI team, the UVA Creative Writing Department and many more.

I am also forever grateful for my family. Thank you to my father for teaching me what a being good man looks like, thank you to my mother for listening and loving and laughing ALWAYS, thank you to Janessa for sharing a room with me for the entirety of COVID summer, and thank you to Melina for helping me find my unexpected love of cross stitching during stressful times. Also thank you for showing no emotion when I said this book is dedicated to you guys. Love that.

And of course, a special thank you to my God. On my own, I am so afraid, but with you I am unapologetically fearless.

Author Bio

Olivia Keenan is an undergraduate student at the University of Virginia pursuing a degree in Biology on a pre-med track. Olivia is from Milwaukee, Wisconsin, where she lives with her parents and two sisters. From a young age, she has been inspired to write about racism and the unique position of being a mixed race Black woman. In high school she was involved in slam poetry and has continued performing spoken word at UVA. Some of the most incredible poets she has ever met come from her college poetry classes and UVA's Flux Poetry club. This is her second shot at writing a poetry book. Her first one *what love does* was a self-published chapbook of which only 50 copies were printed.